YOUR KNOWLEDGE HAS VALUE

AF144779

- We will publish your bachelor's and
  master's thesis, essays and papers

- Your own eBook and book -
  sold worldwide in all relevant shops

- Earn money with each sale

Upload your text at www.GRIN.com
and publish for free

Bibliographic information published by the German National Library:

The German National Library lists this publication in the National Bibliography; detailed bibliographic data are available on the Internet at http://dnb.dnb.de .

Imprint:

Copyright © 2016 GRIN Verlag, Open Publishing GmbH
Print and binding: Books on Demand GmbH, Norderstedt Germany
ISBN: 9783668412514

This book at GRIN:

http://www.grin.com/en/e-book/355109/the-goal-and-process-oriented-approach-in-requirements-engineering

Oliver Götz

The Goal- and Process-Oriented Approach in Requirements Engineering

A Comparison

GRIN Publishing

GRIN - Your knowledge has value

Since its foundation in 1998, GRIN has specialized in publishing academic texts by students, college teachers and other academics as e-book and printed book. The website www.grin.com is an ideal platform for presenting term papers, final papers, scientific essays, dissertations and specialist books.

Visit us on the internet:

http://www.grin.com/

http://www.facebook.com/grincom

http://www.twitter.com/grin_com

The Goal- and Process-oriented Approach in Requirements Engineering – A Comparison

Research Paper

Oliver Götz, University of Cologne

Contents

Introduction

Requirements engineering (RE) is as a subfield of software engineering. It belongs to one of the most fundamental processes in software development as it significantly influences the outcome (Henderson 2006; Panayiotou et al. 2015; Ullah and Lai 2011). It is an iterative process comprising several stages like eliciting, elaborating, structuring, specifying, analyzing and managing the stakeholders' requirements (Daneva and Wieringa 2006). Two methodologies namely process- and goal-oriented RE have been developed to standardize the RE procedure. Process-orientation focuses on the business process itself and how it can be aligned to the existing system (Hill and Wang 2004). Using goal-orientation, the analyst derives goals from requirements mostly looking on non-functional requirements (van Lamsweerde 2001). The achievement of goals is necessary to fulfill the requirement. The mentioned directions are abstract ones, since researchers developed several frameworks, that are derived from them, such as KAOS, TROPOS, i*, NFR etc. (Kavakli 2002; Van Lamsweerde 2000; van Lamsweerde 2001). These approaches can be assigned to either the process- or goal-oriented methods. So in this article, I conduct a comparison of them and create an overview, helping practitioners to pick an appropriate method for their specific contract. Having these frameworks, they support the complete RE procedure and assist to mitigate issues:

Looking at a concrete scenario, namely the implementation of an enterprise resource planning systems (ERP) implementation, RE is a vital task to fulfill the stakeholders' demands and be successful (Panayiotou et al. 2015). Furthermore, occurring stakeholders' conflicts during the requirements specification and inconsistencies are major issues in RE (Cailliau and van Lamsweerde 2013; Daneva and Wieringa 2006; Eveleens and Verhoef 2010; Kavakli 2002; Nguyen et al. 2014; van Lamsweerde 2001). At least two requirements are inconsistent, if they are in opposition to each other, i. e. they cannot be met by the system simultaneously (Nguyen et al. 2014). Hence modifications are necessary to solve the conflict or revoke the inconsistencies. Additionally, occurring issues during the eliciting phase lead to incomplete and inaccurate requirements strengthening this problem area. The analyst and the client work together to develop the requirements (Chakraborty et al. 2015; Chung and Nixon 1995). Each analyst has a different comprehension of the interviewees' utterances, so that misunderstandings and misinterpretations of this kind of qualitative data lead to a vague requirements document. Distributed requirements analysis, i. e. client and vendor not sitting at the same location and therefore have to use tools such as Skype or Lync, is a complication factor as well (Mylopoulos et al. 2002; Mylopoulos et al. 1999; van Lamsweerde 2001).

Therefore, standardized frameworks provide a practical solution to avoid the mentioned problems and I can justify, that a closer look on these kind of approaches is necessary. Hence, my research question is as follows: *What are the current process- and goal-oriented approaches in RE and how do they differ?*

To answer this research question, and based on already conducted research, I carry out a comparative literature review.

I have structured the remainder of this paper as follows. In the first section, I will provide background information about RE and establish important terminology for understanding. In the second section, I describe my research method and its results. In the third section, I illustrate the different RE approaches. In the fourth section, I examine the found approaches looking at differences and similarities by choosing four categories as distinctive features. I wrap up the paper with a conclusion.

Theoretical Background and related Work

Evolution of Requirements Engineering

Looking back in the 90s, researchers hardly focused on RE and thus, little practical advice was available (Panayiotou et al. 2015). However, the few developed approaches address the problem of incomplete RE as mentioned in the introduction (Yu 1997). But, these traditional RE approaches turned out to be inadequate for handling complex information technology (IT) systems such as self-adaptive systems (Nguyen et al. 2014; Rumbaugh et al. 1991). These kind of approaches are somewhat rudimentary and have a narrow perspective in their approach/treatment of RE (Mylopoulos et al. 1999). Requirements engineers conduct system analysis by mixing isolated modeling techniques such as data flow, entity-relationship (ER) and state transition diagrams (van Lamsweerde 2001). Consequently, they were able to collect information that had to be understood, modeled and analyzed before the actual system development phase can start. Nevertheless, they include a couple of drawbacks apart from the shortage of integration (Mylopoulos et al. 1999). They do not capture the fundamental principle, i. e. they lack a detailed view. For example, the analysis elicits the requirement 'security'. Now here are the questions: "What kind of security? Data security or data backup? Fingerprint, password, eye-scanner? Etc.". Consequently, this makes it even more aggravating to set a linkage to high-level concerns in the problem area (Mylopoulos et al. 2002; Nguyen et al. 2014). Additionally, most of the methods consider the modeling and the specification process of a software as singular without taking into consideration interdependencies with the environment (Rumbaugh et al. 1991).

However, traditional methodology does not meet the demands of present day RE due to lack of standardized analyzing methods. On the one hand, systems became more complex. On the other hand, the stakeholders' qualitative data is unstructured and brings inconsistencies as well as constraints along (Doerr et al. 2005). Due to the high influence of object-oriented programming in the last years, the perspective on RE has undergone a change. Research activities more intensively concentrate on the "how to design" question on RE in sense of improvement and alignment with business processes. Furthermore, system integration also plays a significant role in the system development research domain (Doerr et al. 2005; Giorgini et al. 2005; Mylopoulos et al. 1999). Although the dynamic environment is a complex construct, new approaches encourage to explicitly consider those aspects, since they significantly emboss the output (Mylopoulos et al. 1999).

The process- and goal-oriented approach

Examining the existing body of literature and hence to encounter the problems mentioned above, researchers developed two main approaches. These, known as process- and goal-oriented approach, consider the dynamic of the environment and provide holistic techniques to develop requirements for a proposed system (Panayiotou et al. 2015; van Lamsweerde 2001). In order to promote the understanding of both, the process- and goal-oriented approach, requirements and goals should be defined and distinguished from each other:

Usually, requirements are derived from qualitative data, for example from interviews with stakeholders. There are functional as well as non-functional requirements. Functional ones define the task a feature has to do. Non-functional ones are quality attributes which promote e.g. usability, performance, security, portability etc. (Chung and Leite 2009; Hill and Wang 2004; Mylopoulos et al. 1999). Non-functional requirements are not always complementary, they may also be contrary. For example, a credit card system has to process online transactions (the task) in an accurate, secure, fast and user-friendly way (quality attributes). Security is absolutely necessary since without a high degree of security, the user is exposed to the danger of abuse. A highly implemented secure mechanism requires more processing time, because several numbers have to be put in the graphical user interface (GUI) and thus, decelerates the whole process, also affecting the user-friendliness (Haley et al. 2008).

In general usage, goal is associated with facts that have to be achieved at a certain point in the future. From a RE perspective, goals represent organizational objectives or targets having to be fulfilled and for implementing business targets, goal modeling initializes the whole process (Ullah and Lai 2011; van Lamsweerde 2001). Furthermore, goals can be separated into hard- and soft-goals. On the one hand, hard-goals specify functional and on the other hand, soft-goals itemize non-functional requirements (van Lamsweerde 2001). Both of them help to make the requirements operationalizable (Chung and Leite 2009). Defining goals are a key task in the RE process, since they provide a couple of benefits:

1. Generally, achieving a RE completeness is a major concern. Goals represent a precise criterion for an adequate completeness of a requirement. Having a set of goals for the requirements specification, they have the capability to achieve the specification, if all goals are able to be proved (Kavakli 2002).
2. Making requirements understandable for stakeholders is another existing concern. Requirements need a rationale and this is represented by goals. Especially in the business application systems, goals are qualified to set the link between the system-to-be to business and organizational contexts (van Lamsweerde 2001).

Having clarified the two prevailing terms, I can characterize the process- and goal-oriented approach.

Process-oriented requirements engineering (PORE) helps to justify design decisions during the software decision process. According to Mylopoulos et al. (2002) "it attempts to develop formal definitions of non-functional requirements so that a software can be evaluated as to the degree to which it meets its requirements". Since this is a quite narrow definition, I append the following statement to the definition to cover by findings: "PORE also focuses on how business processes can be streamlined with each other and to integrate new ones without violating existing ones in the organization". PORE methodology is usually applied in the context of enterprise resource planning systems (ERP) implementation, especially to align the cross-organizational processes. On the one hand, each company has to be able to manage its own processes. On the other hand, they have to be made transparent, so that they are visible to each stakeholder of the overall enterprise (Daneva and Wieringa 2006; Nguyen et al. 2014).

In contrast to PORE, Goal-oriented requirements engineering (GORE) "is concerned with the use of goals for eliciting, elaborating, structuring, specifying, analyzing, negotiating, documenting, and modifying requirements" (Nguyen et al. 2014). The idea behind is, that a goal tree is constructed which is derived from the requirements. It is possible that they may be related to object models, since goal formulations have a linkage to specific objects such as entities, agents and relationships (Dardenne et al. 1993). As a matter of fact, the examined system is usually analyzed in its operational, technical and organizational setting (Van Lamsweerde 2000). In the case of detecting problems, high-level goals can be defined and refined into further sub-goals to address those problems (Van Lamsweerde 2001; Van Lamsweerde et al. 1998). In the next step, analysts elaborate requirements to satisfy the prior defined goals. By iterating this process, other requirements can be elicited. Summing up, GORE approaches provide both a top-down and bottom-up refinement. They quantify the requirements in order to address major issues associated with a lack of the requirements' basis (Kavakli 2002; Kolp et al. 2001; Nguyen et al. 2014).

Research Method

Research Approach Overview

For answering my research question *"What are the current process- and goal-oriented approaches in RE and how do they differ?"*, I conducted a literature review based on the recommendations of Webster and Watson (2002). After that, I present an analytical framework consisting of four distinctive categories to compare process- and goal-oriented approaches. The literature review comprised three steps: (1) initial review, (2) keyword search via LITSONAR, PROQUEST and EBSCOhost, (3) Backward search.

The initial review revealed, that most of the documents deal with RE approaches containing fundamental knowledge about process- as well as goal-oriented strategies. These documents served the purpose to deliver the basis for further analysis.

For getting more detailed information about current methodologies, I made use of search engines such as LITSONAR, PROQUEST and EBSCOhost. In the beginning, I used LITSONAR, which is a meta search tool and accessed by the University of Cologne Network. I wanted to get a general overview of the existing body of literature in requirements engineering referring to process and goal-oriented approaches. At first, I selected the term "requirements engineering". There were over 10 Million results. I extended the search string to "requirements engineering framework" also having more than 10 Million hits. Hence, the necessity of further key words, the usage of smaller tools, had their justification leading to PROQUEST and EBSCOHOST.

Finally, I conducted a backward search with focus on titles containing terms such as "process-oriented" or "goal-oriented". Consequently, I found basic literature about predominant approaches in RE and could investigate them.

Preliminary Results: Keyword Search

Within this context, I used PROQUEST comprising 26 databases. The string "requirements engineering" delivered 92,564 hits. So, I elected an advanced search method by focusing only on "full text" and "peer-reviewed" articles, reducing output and ensuring the papers' quality. There were 3,885 results. A further constraint, concerning the published date, lead to another compression of the results. Since requirements engineering is an up-to-date research topic as mentioned in the introduction, I filtered only articles published between 2005 and 2015, ended up in 1,744 papers. In order to get more information about process and goal-oriented approaches in requirements engineering, I added the term "framework", i. e. "requirements engineering AND framework". I could minimize the output to 177. Subsequently I extended the string to "requirements engineering AND framework AND software" to get 85 results being more topic-related. Finally, I appended the composite search string with terms within the research question resulting in "requirements engineering AND framework AND (process-oriented OR goal-oriented)". I got 5 hits.

Finally, I caught out the same procedure with EBSCOhost running through 39 databases. I depicted the overall result in table 1, whereas the first value relates to PROQUEST (PR) and the second one to EBSCOhost (EB).

Table 1. Literature review results.				
Search string	Result PR/EB	Constraint		
		Full text	Peer reviewed	2005-2015
"requirements engineering"	92,564/139,814			
"requirements engineering"	3,885/58,764	X	X	
"requirements engineering"	1,744/44,607	X	X	X
"requirements engineering AND framework"	177/3,405	X	X	X
"requirements engineering AND framework AND software"	85/783	X	X	X
"requirements engineering AND framework AND ((process-oriented) OR (goal-oriented))"	5/26	X	X	X

Table 1. Literature review results.

Analytical research framework

Based on my reading, I derived certain attributes that each RE approach has in common (Giunchiglia et al. 2002; Hill and Wang 2004; Mylopoulos et al. 2002; Nguyen et al. 2014; Van Lamsweerde 2000). Firstly, a RE approach consists of a certain analysis technique. Secondly, it uses a special notation to make it standardized and applicable for each analyst. Thirdly, it follows a fundamental principle to achieve a certain goal. Fourthly, there exists not only advantages but also disadvantages, making a RE methodology more or less appropriate for a modeling scenario.

Table 2. Analyzed dimensions.	
Dimension	**Leading question**
Kind of analysis/Context	What kind of analysis is used such as static or dynamic and in which case are they used?
Notation	Which notation is used, for example business modelling language (BPM)?
Rational	What is the fundamental principle behind it, for example business alignment?
Advantages/Disadvantages of GORE and PORE	What are the pros and cons?

Table 2. Analyzed dimensions.

Results

Overview of RE Approaches

In this section, I provide an overview of existing approaches with respect to process- and goal-oriented methodologies. It is not eligible for completeness, since otherwise and due to lack of space, I would have to extend the literature review procedure. Figure 1 illustrates the identified approaches and table 2 puts a more precise view on them. In table 3, I go into more detail by describing the found frameworks which helps to understand the analysis.

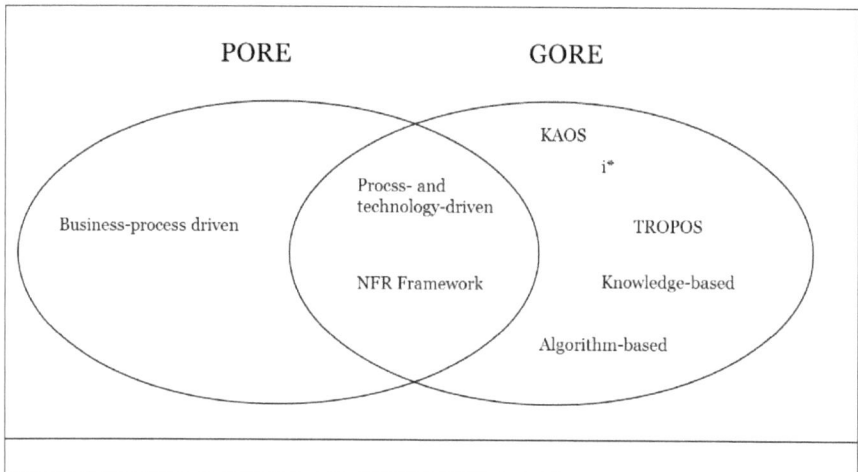

Figure 1: Identified PORE and GORE approaches.

ID	Approach	Characterization	Reference	Membership	
				Process-oriented	Goal-oriented
1	Business-driven	-focus on business processes -using current data from the systems	Ma and Jiang (2014)	X	

Table 3. Overview of found RE approaches.

2	NFR framework	-focuses on the refinement of qualitative requirements into quantifiable ones -refers to the execution, application domain and component architectures	Doerr et al. (2005) Hill and Wang (2004) Mylopoulos et al. (2002) Chung and Nixon (1995)	X	X
3	i*	-agent-oriented -consisting of the components Strategic Dependency and Strategic Rationale -dependency links are modeled between each agents' goals -modeling of system-to-be and organizational environment	Chung and Leite (2009) van Lamsweerde (2001) Bresciani et al. (2004)		X
4	TROPOS	-derived from i* -agent-oriented -holistic framework comprising all stages during a software development process	Bresciani et al. (2004) Giunchiglia et al. (2002) Kolp et al. (2001) Chung and Leite (2009)		X
5	KAOS	-derived from i* -agent-oriented -collection of object,	Van Lamsweerde et al. (1998) Chung and Leite (2009)		X

		goal modelling			
6	Hybrid approach combining technology-driven and process-driven	-business- and technology-driven -focuses on the design process and alignment of business processes with the organization	Daneva and Wieringa (2006) Panayiotou et al. 2015)	X	X
7	Knowledge based	-builds up on KAOS -uses description logic -refers to experience and knowledge	Nguyen et al. (2014)		X
8	Algorithm-based	-builds up on the NFR framework -provides an algorithm to prioritize NFRs after being elicited	Thakurta (2013)		X

Table 3. Overview of found RE approaches.

Discussion

Comparison of RE Approaches

As presented in the prior section, there exists an amount of frameworks being assignable to either the generic process- or goal-oriented approach. In this section, I compare these two approaches by using the four categories that I have introduced in the research method section.

Kind of analysis/Context

Process-oriented approaches use a static analysis method, such as data flow or state transition diagrams, since the dynamics of the environment are being neglected. E. g. engineers specify requirements of the software as a stand-alone system and thus, a connection to the environment is missing (Nguyen et al. 2014). They focus on the business process itself and data flows (K1, K2). A business process comprises several activities and adds value to a prior specified output. The analysts prepare lists with requirements that have to be fulfilled so that the implementation can start. Apart from that, a process oriented method can also look at interdependencies by taking the already existing systems of the organization into account (K3). In that case, the engineers try to streamline the derived requirements to other functionalities so that the system integration is smoothly executable.

Goal-oriented approaches focus less on the functional but more on the non-functional requirements (K4). Their goal is to capture the non-functional requirements (NFR) for the domain of interest and try to decompose them in pieces to make them operationalizable. Furthermore, they explicitly consider the dynamic environment, tradeoffs and ambiguities in their modeling process (K5).

Table 4. Suitable literature references for category "kind of analysis/context".			
Approach	**Representative Quotation**	**ID**	**Summary**
Process-oriented	"...emphasize that how businesses produce their products and services..." (Ma and Jiang 2014)	K1	• Focus on the business process itself • Alignment of processes
	"...a process orientation in an inter-organizational ERP context means predisposing each company [...] to manage itself along its own business processes..." (Daneva and Wieringa 2006)	K2	
	"...the hybrid approach (ERP adaptation to organization and process adjustments to ERP functionality) which can improve the effectiveness of requirements engineering and eventually ERP implementation..." (Panayiotou et al. 2015)	K3	

Goal-oriented	"...the goal of the framework is to put non-functional requirements foremost in developer's mind ..." Chung et al. (2000)	K4	• Consideration of interdependencies • Focus on quality attributes
	"...dealing with ambiguities, tradeoffs, priorities, and interdependencies..." (Van Lamsweerde 2001)	K5	

Table 4. Suitable literature references for category "kind of analysis/context".

Notation

It is widely spread, that system analysis applies formal languages such as the Business Process Management Notation (BPMN) and Unified Modeling Language (UML) regarding process-oriented modeling (N1).

All goal-oriented approaches make use of SIG, which is a softgoal interdependency graph (N2, N3). Usually these graphs represent softgoals linked with each other through the logical operators AND/OR (figure 2). KAOS uses a highly formalized language. An example is illustrated in figure 3, representing the goal that while a train is moving from one to another location, the doors have to be closed. The knowledge-based solution goes one step further. It introduces description logic to put worth on the knowledge- as well as experience-based domain (N4). A found similarity between the two central approaches is, that both of them apply UML. The business process-approach uses activity diagrams, to display the whole business process, beginning from the input until the output. TROPOS for example comprises UML class diagrams, representing the dependencies between each requirement and goal. Being agent-oriented, the technique makes use of state transition and activity diagrams to model the agents' actions.

Table 5. Suitable literature references for category "notation".			
Approach	**Representative Quotation**	**ID**	**Summary**
Process-oriented	"Process models are specified using dedicated process modeling methods - such as the Business Process Modeling Notation (BPMN)..." (Recker et al. 2009)	N1	• Use of formal languages • Sequence diagrams
	"Description logics (DLs) are a family of knowledge representation languages which are decidable subsets of first-order logic." (Nguyen et al. 2014)	N2	
Goal-oriented	"... goals are organized into a goal graph structure, very much in the spirit of AND/OR trees used problem solving." (Mylopoulos et al. 2002)	N3	• Goas trees with AND/OR operations • Graph as visualization tool
	"KAOS introduces AND/OR operationalization links..." (Van Lamsweerde 2001)	N4	

Table 5. Suitable literature references for category "notation".

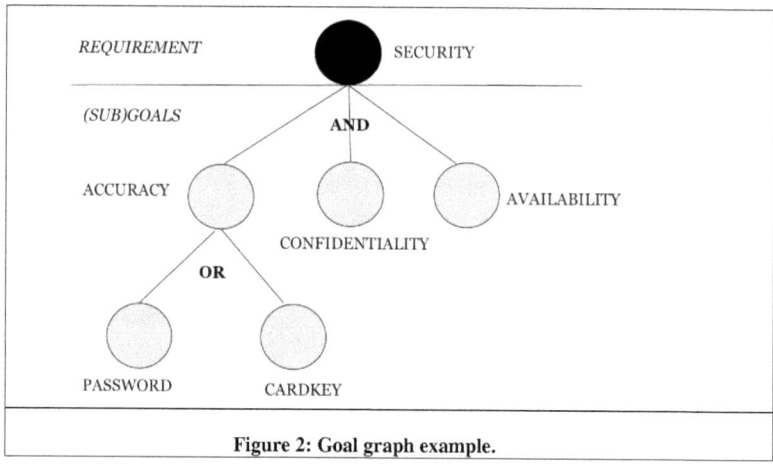

Figure 2: Goal graph example.

$$\{\{\text{for all tr: Train, loc, loc,': Location At (tr,loc) or o At (tr,loc) or o At (tr,loc') or loc} <> \text{loc'} => \text{tr.Doors='closed' or o (tr.Doors='closed')}\}\}$$

Figure 3: Mathematical expression in KAOS.

Rationale

The fundamental principle, both approaches build on, refers to standardization as well as acceleration of the RE procedures. They sharpen the mind for the symbiosis of functional and non-functional requirements. Using UML as mentioned above, the approaches provide a model of the system-to-be. Process-oriented methods put worth on the business process itself (R1).

All goal-oriented approaches make use of decomposition techniques to illustrate dependencies between objects respectively agents and hence, it is an iterative refinement process (R2). It is a kind of divide and conquer principle, i. e. the problem is dismantled into smaller ones in order to finally solve the great one. Usually, goal-oriented approaches refer to the domain knowledge and experience (R3). Moreover, in contrast to a business-process driven approach, TROPOS has been developed as a framework comprising all software development stages without an isolated view of each of them (R4).

Table 6. Suitable literature references for category "rationale".

Approach	Representative Quotation	ID	Summary
Process-oriented	"framework for refining non-functional requirements and incorporating them into the design process..." (Hill and Wang 2004)	R1	• Focus on the design process • Making the result operationalizable
Goal-oriented	"... responsibility links are introduced to relate the goal and agent submodels." (Van Lamsweerde 2001)	R2	• Explicit consideration of interdependencies • Holistic frameworks, i.e. all phases in a software development lifecycle are regarded
	"In the KBRE model, domain knowledge [...] [is] centralized..." (Nguyen et al. 2014)	R3	
	"The TROPOS methodology is intended to support all analysis and design activities in the software development process..." (Bresciani et al. 2004)	R4	

Table 6. Suitable literature references for category "rationale".

Advantages/Disadvantages of PORE and GORE

First of all, I discuss advantages of both main methodologies. On the one hand, process-oriented approaches highlight the (design) process as core element in RE since it creates value. On the other hand, they intend to align the reengineered business processes to the organizations' set of business processes without causing inconsistency issues. The applied techniques are easy to understand, since the they are on a high-level, i.e. no concrete formalization language is used and the flow charts are transparent. Likewise, in a general sense, goal-oriented methods also benefit from the simplicity of UML, as it is understandable for each of the stakeholders. Algorithms have been developed to prioritize the NFRs that have to be fulfilled. Since the goal-oriented methodology is a refining procedure, there will be one point, that the goals cannot be decomposed any more. In this case, the requirement has fully been disassembled in its components. The requirements engineer has finished and can share it for the implementation process. Moreover, the decomposition in goals enables to seek for the requirements' completeness. The breaking down procedure into subsets promotes the stakeholders' understanding and thus, a verification or a necessary modification can quickly be stated out. Having a look at the KAOS example formulation in figure 3, the statement is quite mathematically written. Mathematics is a formulized and precise language, so that each expert being familiar with the topic is able to interpret it. Hence, an international understanding of the proposed goal is granted and shared-content is facilitated. Being agent-oriented, KAOS and TROPOS enable to set roles and thus, simplifying the modeling of interactions between them.

As far as the drawbacks are concerned, I firstly criticize the process-oriented methodology. These kind of approaches hardly take the changing environment into consideration as well the rationale behind a requirement. Although capturing the complexity of the environment is a difficult task, there is a lack of techniques integrating the dynamics of the outer influence into the modelling process. Just listing all requirements, both functional- as well non-functional ones, without putting them into concrete relationships with each other is predestined for upcoming inconsistencies.

As to goal oriented-approaches, they explicitly consider the organizational environment. Therefore, they ensure that requirements are aligned properly and system integration can be caught out in a frictionless way. Apart from that, the extreme formalization, such as in KAOS in figure 3, causes issues. There is no complete shared understanding, since most stakeholders lack the skills to interpret this kind of mathematical expression. Last but least, bringing i* and TROPOS into the mind, they are very comprehensive frameworks and thus, experts need to be acquired and it has to be balanced, if the cost-benefit ratio is adequate.

Conclusions

Contributions

The major output of my comparative literature review is to present a glimpse into existing process- and goal-oriented approaches. In addition, my work provides a comparison of them for encountering upcoming issues in the requirements engineering procedure. Based on the research objective, my literature review contributes in several ways not only to Information Systems Research (IS) in general but also to the specific area of RE.

Firstly, on account of the different literature review stages, I could identify several process- as well as goal-oriented methodologies. I used graphics and tables to grant a quick overview of them. Then I described each of the approach to promote the understanding of the analysis.

Secondly, through cross-reading of the articles, I derived four distinctive categories to detect differences as well as similarities between them. Both approaches incorporate functional and non-functional requirements with each other. On the one hand, process-oriented techniques focus on the business process itself and how to align them during the design decision procedure. On the other hand, goal-oriented methods concentrate on the "how to design" question, i. e. how the business process can be aligned to the existing set of business processes and how systems can be integrated properly. Furthermore, the construct of goals enables a sufficient criterion for completeness and understanding. It is a divide and conquer principle, i. e. on account of several refinements, small problems can be solved. If all of them are solved, the whole problem is solved at last. Standardization, formulization and UML as prevailing modeling language are embedded in both RE directions. Although these attributes contribute to an inflexibility and abstractness, they made the approaches to frameworks providing a basis for each organization.

Limitations

Since RE is a broad area of research, my study has some limitations. It has to be taken into consideration that I give just an overview of found frameworks and methodologies, but do not provide a detailed analysis of them so that they can be used in practice. Since my literature review bases on very specified strings, the search engine may have excluded a couple of other RE approaches in the result.

Future directions

For making the provided approaches applicable in practice, I recommend to conduct case studies where each methodology is demonstrated. Supposed that research activities focus on one case study, e. g. the development of a customer-relationship-software. Then, it will be recognizable how the approaches work and in what way they differ. Consequently, advantages and drawbacks for this very scenario can be derived. Researchers can extend this method to other scenarios. In addition, the used distinctive features for the comparison are not empirically proven. For example, as another impulse for future research directions, a qualitative research on this topic asking practitioners for differences and similarities regarding PORE and GORE may reveal profound categories.

Summing up, I answered the research question *"What are the current process- and goal-oriented approaches in RE and how do they differ?"* to a large extent. I identified process- and goal-oriented methods and examined subcategories. Dividing the analysis process into four categories helped me to investigate specific differences and similarities.

References

Bresciani, P., Perini, A., Giorgini, P., Giunchiglia, F., and Mylopoulos, J. 2004. "Tropos: An Agent-Oriented Software Development Methodology," *Autonomous Agents and Multi-Agent Systems* (8:3), pp. 203-236.

Cailliau, A., and van Lamsweerde, A. 2013. "Assessing Requirements-Related Risks through Probabilistic Goals and Obstacles," *Requirements Engineering* (18:2), pp. 129-146.

Chakraborty, S., Rosenkranz, C., and Dehlinger, J. 2015. "Getting to the Shalls: Facilitating Sensemaking in Requirements Engineering," *ACM Trans. Manage. Inf. Syst.* (5:3), pp. 1-30.

Chung, L., and Leite, J. 2009. "On Non-Functional Requirements in Software Engineering," in *Conceptual Modeling: Foundations and Applications* Heidelberg: Springer, pp. 363-379.

Chung, L., Nixon, B., Yu, E., and Mylopoulos, J. 2000. *Non-Functional Requirements in Software Engineering.* Kluwer:

Chung, L., and Nixon, B. A. 1995. "Dealing with Non-Functional Requirements: Three Experimental Studies of a Process-Oriented Approach," *Proceedings of the 17th international conference on Software engineering*: ACM, pp. 25-37.

Daneva, M., and Wieringa, R. J. 2006. "A Requirements Engineering Framework for Cross-Organizational Erp Systems," *Requirements engineering* (11:3), pp. 194-204.

Dardenne, A., Van Lamsweerde, A., and Fickas, S. 1993. "Goal-Directed Requirements Acquisition," *Science of computer programming* (20:1), pp. 3-50.

Doerr, J., Kerkow, D., Koenig, T., and Olsson, T. 2005. "Non-Functional Requirements in Industry – Three Case Studies Adopting an Experience-Based Nfr Method," *IEEE International Conference on Requirements Engineering.*

Eveleens, J., and Verhoef, C. 2010. "The Rise and Fall of the Chaos Report Figures," *IEEE software* (27:1), p. 30.

Giorgini, P., Mylopoulos, J., and Sebastiani, R. 2005. "Goal-Oriented Requirements Analysis and Reasoning in the Tropos Methodology," *Engineering Applications of Artificial Intelligence* (18:2), pp. 159-171.

Giunchiglia, F., Mylopoulos, J., and Perini, A. 2002. "The Tropos Software Development Methodology: Processes, Models and Diagrams," in *Agent-Oriented Software Engineering Iii.* Springer, pp. 162-173.

Haley, C. B., Laney, R., Moffett, J. D., and Nuseibeh, B. 2008. "Security Requirements Engineering: A Framework for Representation and Analysis," *Software Engineering, IEEE Transactions on* (34:1), pp. 133-153.

Henderson, P. 2006. "Why Large It Projects Fail," *ACM Trans. Program. Lang. Syst* (15:5), pp. 795-825.

Hill, R., and Wang, J. 2004. "Quantifying Non-Functional Requirements: A Process Oriented Approach," in: *Requirements Engineering Conference*. pp. 1-7.

Kavakli, E. 2002. "Goal Oriented Requirements Engineering: A Unifying Framework," *Requirements Engineering* (6:4), pp. 237-251.

Kolp, M., Giorgini, P., and Mylopoulos, J. 2001. "A Goal-Based Organizational Perspective on Multi-Agent Architectures," in *Intelligent Agents Viii*. Springer, pp. 128-140.

Ma, Q., and Jiang, Y. 2014. "Process-Oriented Information System Requirements Engineering-a Case Study," *Journal of Business Cases and Applications* (10), p. 1.

Mylopoulos, J., Chung, L., and Nixon, B. 2002. "Representing and Using Nonfunctional Requirements: A Process-Oriented Approach," *IEEE Transactions on Software Engineering* (18:6), pp. 483-497.

Mylopoulos, J., Chung, L., and Yu, E. 1999. "From Object-Oriented to Goal-Oriented Requirements Analysis.," *Communications of the ACM* (42:1), pp. 31-37.

Nguyen, T. H., Vo, B. Q., Lumpe, M., and Grundy, J. 2014. "Kbre: A Framework for Knowledge-Based Requirements Engineering," *Software Quality Journal* (22:1), pp. 87-119.

Panayiotou, N. A., Gayialis, S. P., Evangelopoulos, N. P., and Katimertzoglou, P. K. 2015. "A Business Process Modeling-Enabled Requirements Engineering Framework for Erp Implementation," *Business Process Management Journal* (21:3), pp. 628-664.

Recker, J. C., zur Muehlen, M., Siau, K., Erickson, J., and Indulska, M. 2009. "Measuring Method Complexity: Uml Versus Bpmn," Association for Information Systems.

Rumbaugh, J., Blaha, M., Premerlani, W., Eddy, F., and Lorensen, W. E. 1991. *Object-Oriented Modeling and Design*. Prentice-hall Englewood Cliffs, NJ.

Thakurta, R. 2013. "A Framework for Prioritization of Quality Requirements for Inclusion in a Software Project," *Software Quality Journal* (21:4), pp. 573-597.

Ullah, A., and Lai, R. 2011. "Modeling Business Goal for Business/It Alignment Using Requirements Engineering," *Journal of Computer Information Systems* (51:3), pp. 21-28.

Van Lamsweerde, A. 2000. "Requirements Engineering in the Year 00: A Research Perspective," *Proceedings of the 22nd international conference on Software engineering*: ACM, pp. 5-19.

Van Lamsweerde, A. 2001. "Goal-Oriented Requirements Engineering: A Guided Tour," *Fifth IEEE International Symposium on IEEE*, pp. 249-262.

Van Lamsweerde, A., Darimont, R., and Letier, E. 1998. "Managing Conflicts in Goal-Driven Requirements Engineering," *Software Engineering, IEEE Transactions on* (24:11), pp. 908-926.

Webster, J., and Watson, R. T. 2002. "Analyzing the Past to Prepare for the Future: Writing a Literature Review," *MIS Quarterly* (26:2), pp. 13-23.

Yu, E. S. 1997. "Towards Modelling and Reasoning Support for Early-Phase Requirements Engineering," *Requirements Engineering, 1997., Proceedings of the Third IEEE International Symposium on*: IEEE, pp. 226-235.